THUNDER ALLEY

Cover Image: Blackburn Streetplan, 1848

Frontispiece: Gandhi's 1931 visit to the cotton workers of Darwen,
near Blackburn, at the time of the Indian boycott of Lancashire cotton.

Cover and author photographs by Rebecca Chesney:
www.rebeccachesney.com

First published in Great Britain in 2008 by
Aussteiger Publications, 21 Lowergate, Clitheroe, Lancashire, BB7 1AD
Aussteiger_211@hotmail.com

Reprinted May 2009

Designed by Craig Birtles: craigbirtles@yahoo.co.uk
Printed by Lamberts Print & Design, Settle, North Yorkshire

The author acknowledges the generous
support of the Arts Council of England.

A CIP catalogue record for this book is available from the British Library

ISBN: 978 18727641 46

THUNDER ALLEY

Sonnets and Other Poems

Mark Ward

AUSSTEIGER PUBLICATIONS

Mark Ward was born in Blackburn. He has worked on Alaskan radio, built film sets in Africa and worked for a New Zealand production company. He has been the recipient of several writers awards.

He has written numerous collections of poetry and prose, most recently, *Used Rhymes* (2007, Aussteiger Publications) and *A Guide to Historic Haworth & the Brontës* (2007, Hendon Publishing).

For Tanya

ACKNOWLEDGEMENTS

Richard Stanton, Matthew Hollis, Mark Bains, Catherine Kay, Will Carr, Ann Lambert, Craig Birtles, Rebecca Chesney, the late Robert Woof, Dad: for his stories, Joe Cudden, the Arts Council of England, David Wilson, the staff of the Wordsworth Trust; and all the good folks of Blackburn and Grasmere.

Huge thanks to Paul Farley and Neil Rollinson.

CONTENTS

Regret, 7

Time Zones, 8

Specimens, 9

Junction 31, 10

Regret ii, 11

Mr Mercer leaves his Wife,12

Mr Brown goes to Colwyn. 13

Mrs Eccles walks on Air, 14

Regret iii,15

Thunder Alley, 16

   i Cycles

   ii Home-grown

   iii The last supper

   iv Victimization

Regret iv, 20

Spinning Jenny, 21

Polish Barber, 22

Umbilical Cord, 23

Regret v, 24

Landfill, 25

Michael Dixon, 26

Legends, 27

Regret vi, 28

Killers, 29

Days like These, 30

The Mansion of Aching Hearts, 32

Regret vii, 33

Shadows, 34

Itchy Coo, 35

Amusements, 36

Regret viii, 37

Church Candle, 38

November, 39

You could be Anywhere, 40

Regret ix, 41

Thou shalt be . . . Nothing, 42

Blakewater, 43

An Eventful Night, 44

Regret x, 45

T, 46

Kingfisher, 47

Oh and by the way . . . , 48

I'll be out of here
before the first blank ice, well before rotten
gutters grow healthy fangs.

Geoffrey Hill

FOREWORD

I once had a friend with whom I'd discuss writing. His was a dangerous mind, full of brilliant insights, and as we sat up drinking rivers of whiskey and eating crackers, I would greedily listen. An ever-present part of his mind was Wordsworth, and he would frequently talk of the notion that poetry is 'a man talking to men,' playing with the neat singular / plural opposition and, after a sip of whiskey, adding 'whether they're in the same room, or thousands of years apart.' It is one of the greatest truths about poetry, almost self-evident, and it stuck.

When I was asked to write a foreword to *Thunder Alley*, and had begun reading the manuscript, the poems brought that truth back to my mind. They have a clear, strong voice, and speak directly to the reader. In a world where the word 'poetry' typically causes fearful glances and a lull in conversation, where it is seen as an inaccessible art form written and read by a small self-styled elite, this book is refreshingly free of the problems and the baggage of definition. Whether teasing Geoffrey Hill's sense of apocalyptic scale, or remembering a young friend's painful accident, these poems are wide-ranging, lucid, and distinctly one man's work, one man's imagination, and one man's reflections.

That is not to deny their universality, quite the contrary. There is a great sense for the things that matter in our minds – home, friends, the past, the future – and all of the pushing and pulling in life. But whether it's the shrewish home of Mr Mercer that he escapes from beautifully or the worlds apart illuminated by a cigarette in 'Junction 31', for every disappointment, every sawdust bedsit with roaches underneath the fridge, there is an elation at community, commonality. It might be about the place you grew up, or the desire to rewrite the past despite ourselves. Poems like 'Mrs Eccles Walks on Air' show a kindred spirit, someone else aware of those magical flights of fantasy that can begin where you are most grounded, inspired and lifted by the world you were then a part of. There is intelligence, but also something far more important: warmth. The author is an interested observer, never afraid of an opinion or a statement of the obvious, and that makes them graceful monuments to the modern condition.

Yet: that's not to say that this book is in any way about the better sides of human nature, or even optimistic. People are driven by fear as much as hope, and the 'Thunder Alley' sequence that the book is structured around is unflinching and forensic about the darker side of society – the lies we tell ourselves to avoid confronting a situation, the one-track mind that can lead to obsession and destruction, the horrible consequences of thoughtless actions. They are not easy poems to read, because we know this world, from the friend who got into a fight with the wrong people in a nightclub, to the news we see every day.

It is a book about specific places and people, and about everyone's mind, a book that turns a keen and far-reaching eye on the worlds we each live in and invent for ourselves, a book about the private tragedies and triumphs of a life. The thousands upon thousands of tender folds in the mind that conceal innumerable personal reflections are each our own, and this book's subject. They are stubbornly human in the face of inhumanity, and infused with that

4

hint of the Romantic, where even as despair and emptiness is faced unflinchingly they rage utterly against the dying of the light. They are full of horror stories, pain, suffering, and delusions, not below the odd bit of gallows humour; and they are full of happiness, freedom; the imagination of a better world.

And how could any introduction neglect to mention the 'Regrets' that punctuate the poems, alternately funny and bittersweet, offering their more immediate pleasures while subtly reinforcing the structure of the book – alerting the reader to both a finished inspiration and a work-in-progress. We are aware of the poems as written records, protean until fixed on the page. It is at once an affirmation of the power of print, but with a sly nod to impermanence, change, and the author's constant desire to improvise and revise.

Finishing this book, I reread it, and days later, was still thinking about many lines within it. The book comes together to form a complete picture of a man's mind, and has the quality of memorable speech: the sounds of *Thunder Alley* and Mark Ward intermingle, and you feel they are in the same room, talking. I like Mark Ward, I like the sound of his voice. I had had thoughts of co-opting Wordsworth into ending this introduction, tying it up in a neat and canonical bow. But ultimately *Thunder Alley* is here, speaking for itself and proudly independent: you could not ask for more from a book of poems.

Richard Stanton

Regret

A Question

When the ice-shelf shifts.
What's going to happen to
all the ornaments?

Time Zones

New Delhi: 5am – Dawn's first light seeks
the homeless and dispossessed, and for
a moment at least the day belongs to them . . .

Driving from the city to the airport,
the hundreds of ragged bundles lining
the embankments were stirring to life,
as a warm sun gently announced itself.
Men lit kerosene stoves and made tea,
while women washed their babies in the drains.
The cold grey suds honeycomb and disperse,
dissolving into ditches alongside.

Blackburn: 8am – The morning sun backlights
the curtains, revealing Indian Cottons
tightly woven threads, of independence.

Specimens

Hobart: The colonial artists generally
depicted the Aboriginals, now extinct;
as a naked, ignorant sub-species,
lacking intelligence and common decency.

Propped in a box inside a specimen case,
a rare photograph of few survivors
of the 'Black War,' exiled to Flinders Isle
told a different story. Awkwardly
dressed in ill-fitting western clothes, they are
haunted and frightened; their lives fragmented,
their history about to be erased,
they stare out from the fading image like ghosts.

Joining them on display – a glass-eyed tiger; extinct:
and corset stays – made from albatross wings.

Junction 31

Airport Taxis

There may be a no smoking policy
but these Asian guys are usually ok?
All right if I smoke mate? Been a hell of a flight.
'No problem: been anywhere interesting?'
Kashmir, I tell him. He ponders a moment.
'Indian or Pakistan?' *Indian.*
'Aah . . .' We both fall silent and return.
I to the campfires, the saffron pickers,
and the Floating Gardens of Srinagar,
he to the daily shelling, the terror,
confusion, loss and enforced separation.
On the road, always moving – even now,
each long mile, taking him further away.

It's Junction 31 mate. Almost home.

Regret ii

Haiku to the Fairground Goldfish

Clear plastic to black,
in usually less than
a week – Assured.

Mr Mercer leaves his Wife

The mealy-mouthed Mercer flies his kite,
when summer's luscious sparkling rain abates.
And the tarmac and the red brick and the slates,
are swilled and spilled with gold and silver light,
which shines on Mrs Mercer's polished face.
All buffed and waxed and plucked and pinched and preened.
She scowls and says, 'The sun should know his place
to shine so uninvited on One he should esteem!'
Her husband, cowed, replied he couldn't say.
His soaring kite, whorled, wheeled and dipped and spun.
As she loathed him with a look and turned away,
Mr Mercer and the kite became as One.

He sees the sunlight liquefy his spouse,
and altitude reduce her, 'til at last:
she was a resin-coated insect – with his house
a lump of amber, set in a silver clasp.

Mr Brown goes to Colwyn

His pastime – since the war left him disabled:
Splayed fingers, palms flat, sweeping the pieces
in two opposing arcs across the table,
he sorted sea from sky, and other features.

With a surgeon's innate skill and application,
he attached a coast to Cymru's brooding hills.
Finding deep in his imagination,
a cathartic joining of his shattered limbs.

White sky: white splintered shards of bone, he fused
together, his thumb pressing, smoothing every fracture.
Foregoing both his frame and fitted shoes,
to run on Colwyn's sands, in all-consuming rapture.

For that one moment he was briefly man *and* boy,
until the tide redeemed his gladness and his sorrow,
the footprints formed of leaping boundless joy;

The Zimmer's puncture holes – the trailed foot furrow.

Mrs Eccles walks on Air

'Got you, you little rascal!' she rasped and,
removing the broom-handle from my back wheel,
prodded me as I lay tangled in the bike.
'That'll teach you not to ride around here!'

Later, the smell of Dettol; and dark thoughts
about the old crow, pervaded my dreams.
Once more she thrust the broom: Then the strangest thing,
as it somehow lodged underneath the seat.
With her bird-like hands gripping the shaft
and her petticoats a-swish, she was
dragged bouncing and shrieking along the road.

What joy and delight as the children sang . . .

Tra-la-la-lee – There goes Mrs Eccles.
Dragged down the street like a Witch to the gallows.
Lets hope it's a good rope, strong and thick.
Put her in a noose and beat her with a stick.

Regret iii

Roaches

I've stayed in some shit-holes in my time,
but that bedsit in Munich takes some beating.

Coming home one night I saw the fridge move!
– Not as in physically moving across the floor:
More like, it was trembling where it stood,
over by the window.
I switched on the light to find every part
of its surface, covered with small brown cockroaches,
of the North European variety.
A mass so dense it seemed to move as one.

You just wouldn't expect it of the Germans.

Thunder Alley

I

Cycles

Unprompted, he can casually dispense
a razor to the cheek of innocence,
carving his problems in his victim's face:
a white-bone pelmet, a sagging crimson drape.

Whenever he gets troubled, bored or stressed,
a gasbag brings him temporary oblivion.
The girl he meets is suitably impressed,
and he fucks her in the park by the pavilion.

At fifteen, she's pregnant with his child.
He gifts her a bracelet and some trainers,
ignores her when his hooded mates are round,
and kicks her for the slightest misdemeanour.

'Things will improve when the baby arrives,'
she tells herself, tasting his boot in her mouth.

Home-grown.

It is important when passing through this life
to leave some record of ones journey.

Thomas Gray

Fairly straightforward this martyrdom thing:
Blind faith: Semtex and a ticket one-way.
Where to? Well that's entirely down to physics.

This elegy records his earthly stay.

He could have been a doctor or lawyer.
A teacher; someone held in high esteem.
He never realized his full potential.
Full many a flower was born to blush unseen.

His life was brief and unremarkable.
He died abroad with malice in his heart,
dispatched among the scorched and carbonised,
the guiltless amputees with shattered lives.
Formless; reduced to ounces, blood and fat
slather on the walls of a Tel-Aviv bar.

The Last Supper

Remember the 70s; the Skinheads,
the Sex Pistols; Carlos the Jackal,
mayhem on the terraces: the three-day week.
Picketing gravediggers, blackouts and bombs.
The I.R.A was toasting its success
while some poor bastard was getting his head
kicked in, for his simply being Irish;
and not for anything he'd done or said.
And spare a thought for Jimmy McGuerter.
On his way home with a fish supper in
the aftermath of Mountbatten's murder . . .

They punched and kicked him so hard that his head
burst open on the pavement like a ripe fruit.

His subsequent meals – ingested through tubes.

Victimization

The fat kid with the jam-jars always copped
it. Or those too clever, beautiful or black,
or gay, or just plain different – their riposte;
to learn self-ridicule – or join the pack.
Those too shy or lacking self-esteem,
and often friends with whom they might confide,
could find each day a harrowing ordeal.
Tormented to the verge of suicide.
And racism itself is non-exclusive.
The fat kid with the jam-jars understands:
As one we are generous and inclusive.
As tribes we seem by nature, partisan.

When our streets form galleries of commonwealth.
Through every painted frame you see yourself.

Regret iv

The Editor

For Paul Farley

42 poems: *A modest collection,*
I told myself,
handing them over.

24 poems – *A pamphlet perhaps?*
He suggests
handing them back!

Spinning Jenny

At the dance of '63 for working folk,
where Carders, Weavers, Winders, Spinners all;
piss-stinking Fullers with raw ammonia sores;
were starched and groomed for the annual Summer Ball.

The dancers themselves were cumbersome and tired.
Their automatons mimicking their toils.
And leaden wooden clogs with horseshoe irons,
ground and crunched the flags in the Village Hall.

Everything they'd ever known then changed,
as barefoot from the shadows stepped a girl.
They stood in horror; wonderment, amazed;
transfixed: – as she began to slowly turn.
Then faster, faster still, as on a wheel
– Or spool, yet oh so graceful and succinct.
Through Time and generations she revealed . . .

A world engulfed in smoke and dust and lint.

The Polish Barber

A modest man by nature: stoic; dignified
for many years he'd lived in Blackburn town.
Haunted by an incident; so vivid, so profound
– one evening with my father he broke down . . .

His tears found tributaries in his face,
coursed through deltas clawed by gulags and the reek
of the airless cattle-trucks with the displaced,
to form a pool within the socket of his cheek.

He sees his harried village ringed by tanks,
as men with bayonets despoil the land.
And his brother swinging lifeless from a lamp –
post, his woollen trousers stained with shit and
semen, his battered body spat on and defiled,
the laughing Russian soldiers drinking beer.
And he a witness: Just a helpless child,
that day: Then every night for thirty years.

Umbilical Cord

They've never crushed the pillow at my side.
Nor pushed the air when entering my space.
And reassuring words I've been denied,
from those without a likeness or a face.
Breath so cold no mammal could survive
that icy fog: behind the unseen caul,
a powdered box with rags; and calcified,
the remains of those in me that came before.

A cord transparent, yet 10 times 10 thousand
chains, that man or men have ever made
in strength; draws me through the wakeful hours,
and distant lands, bringing me back again.

To Pleasington, where the dead converge,
in silent rows, repentant, unconcerned.
An oblong scar, a Remembrance Book page;

a dimple in the earth, above an urn.

Regret v

Spanish Lament

When I was a kid
they returned with sombreros.
Sangria and castanets;
lacquered lace fans.

Now it's a villa.
A Timeshare apartment:
Skin melanomas.
Booze and cheap fags.

Landfill

Old Tom Barker down at the landfill
slept with a fireguard over his head
to prevent the rats from chewing his lobes.
Had his whiskers bleached white by their urine instead,
as they to'd and fro'd across the bridge, spanning his face.

Uncle Jack washed his hair in paraffin
to prevent lice. To which it could be regarded
a success – as it also prevented hair growth.

Aunty Molly thought we'd sent a boatload
of gherkins to the Falklands: She always misheard.
When Lord Ha Ha said the Palace was a target.
She thought he meant *The Palace* where she worked.

Bernard died, but kept walking by Alice's window.
He wouldn't leave until she joined him – so she did.

Michael Dixon

Scrawny lad with orange hair, (the type that
doesn't like the sun:) a keen fisherman,
he preferred the river bends to street corners
and bus shelters, where his mates would hang out.

When all hell broke loose in the nightclub and
he was singled out for 'a good kicking'
by the doormen – his skinny ribs couldn't take it.

He got through the night, but the next day on
the river – he started drifting –

                         down –

                             down,

by the sloping banks of the long green water:
the hot blue lights and the black asphalt:
past the cool white sheets and hurried voices;
through the rising vapours at the distant bar;
and on – to the eternal sea beyond.

Legends

I keep seeing him: Captain Cook, that is.
He's there now: mute bronze; at his *Anchorage,*
looking out over a stretch of water
he named in frustration, *Turnagain Arm;*
while attempting to find the North West Passage.

She's there too: The Sleeping Lady,
rising out of the sea, like a mountain.
He'd lost his way – but she'd lost her heart.

Waiting in vain for her man to return,
she'd lain down to sleep by the water's edge.
The snow fell, and the ice formed about her.
Moulding to her, it replicated her
in repose: her hair a dignified white.

She waits still: along with the mute Captain.
Both are contemplative: both immortal.
His towering achievement – Her deep love.

Regret vi

Impulse

For Will

In the process of writing
my Grant Proposal, I
smoked some boogie-ball.

Out of focus – the words spread
across the page like bacteria . . .

And I found myself . . . Unworthy.

Killers

There are some things that just stay with you.
Seeing distressed dogfish abort live young on the
deck of a trawler: While the boatman ripping
the hook from the cod's mouth outlasted the taste.

Saw a gut-shot possum; whose spewing intestines
hooked on a branch before unravelling in her wake,
as she leapt through the treetops in futile escape,
while I'm screaming: *For Gods sake fucking kill it*!!

I remember Mick wanting to reclaim his hook
from a perch, that had swallowed it,
wrapped the line round his fist, placed his boot on the fish
and tore – dragging out the crimped scarlet hem of its gills.
The dislodged maggot, now threaded like a bead,
and its heart – drowning; still beating on the barb.

Days like These

I

It was auspicious all right – waking up naked,
the room crypt cold: the bedclothes having been
wrested from me in the night, and heaped
on the floor in what seemed a malicious act:
While all the room brooded in abstract shadow.

Dragging back the cover, and rolling myself
up to prevent my unwrapping again,
I began to feel a little claustrophobic . . .
Something wasn't right – even the drizzle on the
window resembled the drawn desperate
fingernails of someone trying to get in:

The day finally arrives, and my uneasiness
seems justified when answering the door:
Might've known . . . on days like these the bailiff calls.

OK, I tell myself, I'm well prepared for this,
when he wants my name – I'll tell him something else.
'Is it Mark, Mark Ward?' he asks – like he already knows it is.
And I find myself agreeing, 'cause I just can't help myself.
'Mr Ward you have a bill, outstanding with B.T.'
Those bastards will get fuck-all out of me!
It was only 97 and now it's 253.
I write him a cheque, to make him go away.

Returning to my room, dejected, appalled
at my performance, after so many rehearsals.
My anxiety intensifies to see
the scrawny fingernails of drizzle from the night,
having transferred to the inside, are now tearing
down the windowpane, desperate to get out.

The Mansion of Aching Hearts

At the former Union Workhouse on the hill,
they'd sit in soporific bliss and stare,
as slanted latticed sunbeams sloped – and spilling
through the windows, split the melancholy air.
Wayne Ruben squints, adjusts his stool,
lines the light-shaft with the table and bench.
Jane will dip her toes, then skirt the pool
of sun: dark shadows more familiar, less intense.

Now the restraining cells are silent, and the halls
where the sectioned were sedated and observed
echo no more with disillusioned souls,
the corridors no longer the preserve
of aching hearts, the dormitories now still,
at the former Union Workhouse on the hill.

Regret vii

First impressions

Interview with Robert Woof, at the Wordsworth Trust.

It had all been going great; then:
Do you drink? 'Well . . . Yes,' I replied.
Smoke? 'Affirmative.'
I was somewhat startled by the questions:
Had I disappointed him already?
No water-drinking bard here:
Just another flawed Coleridgean.

Shadows

He seemed quite normal – unlike the perverts
we'd normally see wandering round the park.
They were easy to spot – bit grubby; bit twitchy.

'Come over here I've got something for you?'
Leaving my friends I followed him into the bushes.
'Now close your eyes and open your mouth.'
I did, but cheated – just as his dick was coming out!
– At which I took off like a greyhound, across
the grass verge and back to the playground.
I wised-up pretty quickly after that.
Avoided shadows; was always ready to run;
and kept his face imprinted on my mind.

He's there still . . ? Mid thirties with short dark hair:
About 5′9″; wearing jeans and a checked shirt.

Itchy Coo . . .

Was unmistakable; with his wide brimmed hat,
thick-rimmed spectacles, and a white beard
that 40 a day had turned the colour of
caramelised sugar, around his mouth.
We assumed him to be a learned man
as he seemed to be constantly reading:
On public benches; at the library;
even on the lunch-walk to Nazareth House.
Then one day he just disappeared
                                    – Nobody
noticed at first: I suppose he'd been part
of the neighbourhood, without ever belonging:
It took a while to register he was missing.

By which time he'd quietly turned the page
and moved on to another chapter . . .

Amusements

I made my money that day, on the Penny Falls,
when my carefully slotted penny brought
down the whole row: momentarily fused,
it crashed hard; like a lump of solid bronze.

Half a pound heavier, and feeling rich,
I made my way up to the Marina,
where a rather sad looking dolphin, waved,
chattered and leapt through hoops, for our amusement.

From there, the Reptile House and its star attraction;
two alligators – in touching distance
through the railings. Bored and uninspired,
they lay motionless by the shallow pool,
every inch of their backs covered in coins,
thrown by frustrated punters wanting action.

Sequined alligators – Now that's showbiz!

Regret viii

Self-Awareness

This infection on my face is proving
to be a marvellous form of contraception.

It's a resilient beast: my top lip,
swollen and pustulating seems to draw the eye
of friends and strangers alike.

It's a malignant bacterium: a trespasser reluctant
to move on . . .
Unwanted and uninvited it has its own agenda,
serving no purpose
other than making me painfully aware
of who I am.

Church Candle

That night, he sacrificed himself for love.
Drawn to the naked flame in search of a mate,
he stumbled into a pool of hot wax,
and there – like a limed finch, he remained.

I found him the next morning: wings outstretched,
opaque: entombed in the central crater.

I re-lit the candle and released him.
Unbound, he floated brightly: his vivid
markings; a glazed umber and chestnut brown,
seemed to ripple in the soft bending light.

And so it continued each night:
                              Until
the well deepened, the high walls collapsed, and
the moth; consumed within an avalanche
of molten wax
                    – was ultimately redeemed.

November

i.m. M. D. Ward

Nothing should grow here, I told myself,
easing my fingers through the thin crust of frost,
into the cold red sand of the fresh grave.

The earth was already compacting – good drainage
they said; though I try not to think about that!
I prefer using my hands to cold steel:
This was no autopsy; more like contact.
The impression of my fingers created
fluted fist-size earthenware bowls,
and into each I placed four bulbs – a nest.

This month I thought we'd keep each other company.
What else is there . . ? An answer phone message:
That look, you gave me at the hospital door:
And this red sand in my fingernails, I'm loath to remove.

You could be Anywhere?

It happens sometimes on really dark nights,
when the orange street lights of Pendle Drive
and Roman Road, seem to float: They remind
me of the fire-boats at anchor on the
Bosphorus: men frying fish in iron skillets.
Taking turns to come quayside with their catch.

Only the other day the morning sun
over Whiteburk, glared with such intensity,
I thought of the bush-fires in New South Wales,
and closed my window to keep out the smoke.

In a misty haze; the rumble of trucks
on Preston New Road is *Mosi O Tunya*,
The Smoke that Thunders; rising as vapour,
from the bowels of Victoria Falls.

Regret ix

Prosthetics

Ben ripped his nuts off, sliding down a flagpole.
Caught them on the cord-hook . . . Ouch!
You couldn't tell the difference when they gave him rubber ones.
Except they had a tendency to bounce.

Thou shalt be... Nothing

Sappho

That Greek bird knew what she was on about!
I too was passed around and displayed for a while.
'He has the look of you they'd say,' laughing,
as even my non-fashion became dated.

As interest waned, I began spending more time
under the stairs in a dusty envelope:
Packed up, moved around and heaped upon.

Then, accidentally left behind in the move.

Not long now to complete anonymity.
Bearing no name and being of no relation
I won't be tolerated down here for long.
My own exile beckons – consigned to a box
in the attic; yellowing; a little parched,
and beginning to curl at the edges.

Blakewater

You couldn't feed the ducks or dip your toes,
King Cotton's needs had sent it underground:
A culvert – Yes; a river – I suppose:
unseen – and sliding deep beneath the town.

Fish couldn't see the stars to navigate
inside the chamber underneath the town,
so ceased the urge to gather and migrate
to the Pennines – their ancient breeding grounds.
Choking, all the fish came up for air,
at King Street by the bone / glue factory,
where kids could get a shilling for rats' tails
and folk could dump their mattresses for free.

In ancient times a group of settlers came;
building farms, then water-powered factories.
Now that from which the town derives its name
lies buried – with its cotton industry.

An Eventful Night

I tell you; it's busy out there tonight!
People everywhere: See my mum as well:
Having dinner with the boxing promoter
Don King – At the Sett End of all places?

Everything's real: nothing's impossible.
Even the blind man is seeing clearly,
while the deaf girl hears him whisper her name,
by the kissing-gate, where she rendezvous.

Yep, it sure is busy: Yet oh so strange.
Everyone is familiar, yet somehow
out of place?
                    Suddenly, seconds later,
there's not a soul about, and I'm clinging
to this ledge, a fingertip from safety,
wondering – Where the fuck is everyone?

Regret x

The Ratchet

For Neil Rollinson

'What's this? Victoriana! I don't hear you
talk like that: It's wrong: get rid, it's out of place.
And tell me: What's with all the fucking adverbs?
This poem carries too much baggage mate!'

T

Those long car journeys were pure quality.
People play i-spy; count Eddie Stobart trucks,
or listen to the radio between
service breaks: Tanya and I – we'd chat.

'So I guess that makes me a fruit salad',
she said, after some deliberation,
having learned that her genetic make-up
took in seven countries and two continents.
That got me thinking:
                            How we're not made-up
of one thing – but many; and that the place
we were born doesn't necessarily
define us. Identities are assumed
and discarded, as we seek out who we are.

The one we come to know and learn to live with.

Kingfisher

For R.C.

Enchanted birds, kingfishers; and like water-sprites
seldom seen in these parts. Yet since I've taken
to walking with you, I've already seen
two: the last one only the other day.

More projectile than vertebrate, his long
beak gives him a severe countenance; this
is more than compensated by his bright
iridescent plumage: robes fit for a king.

We barely noticed the moorhen nearby:
Her modest down by comparison, seemed
quite drab: nor did we audibly gasp when
she shuffled nervously from the reed bed,
as when he flashed across the water like
phosphorous: alighting on the alder beside us.

Where sitting with you, in the late afternoon,
by the sloe-black river – everything was perfect.

Oh, and by the way . . .

I like you; I like the sound of your voice:
The deep resonance, of your earthy vowels.
Coarse, salty, yet familiar as the moist
dank air, and coal smoke seeping through rooftop cowls.

The Brewery's rancid yeasty breath exhales
and mingles with the clipped consonants – no frills;
just calico, coal and raw cotton bales.
The filthy canal – a great sump for the mills.

Your abbreviated syntax feels like home.
Worn; uneven like the former cobbled lanes.
Hard-pressed forebears interred within the loam.

A broken iron downspout gulps and gurgles in the rain.

Your slow syllabic shuffle glides – and grapples
the larynx; through primary instinct, not choice;
the child, the fairground, the sweet toffee apples,
return and enrich the sound of your voice.